ORAL ROBERTS

Cashing In Your Receipt with God

Tapping Into Your
Heavenly Account

CONTENTS

A Personal Word of Introduction
from Richard Roberts

From the time I was a little boy, I remember my dad teaching me about the biblical principles of seedtime and harvest–about planting my seeds unto the Lord and expecting to receive a harvest back from Him. One of the best things that I learned early was how to give to God *with joy*. I learned that when I gave, I wasn't just throwing my time, my talent, my money–my seed–into the wind, never knowing what would happen. *I could expect* God to multiply the seeds I sowed and grow them into a harvest of miracles for my life.

In the late 1960s, my dad first shared *The Miracle of Seed-Faith* with the world, and I believe it literally revolutionized the way many Christians began to understand that when they gave, they could expect to receive back from the Lord. It has certainly shaped Lindsay's and my life, and the lives of our children and loved ones.

I'm excited about this book my dad has written. I believe the more we learn about how we can tap into our heavenly account with God, the more we can stand in agreement with God's Word in Malachi 3:10-11 and begin to expect such a harvest of blessing in every area of our lives–spiritually, physically, financially, and in our families–from Him, that there will not even be room enough to contain it all.

CHAPTER ONE

A Banker Explains to Me What Receipting Is in the Secular World

As far back as 1947, when I was 29, I realized the Lord was using many things and many people to give me insight and knowledge concerning giving and receiving, sowing and reaping. God showed me His divine plan for whole-person prosperity as He had set it up for His kingdom on this earth–especially from the standpoint of "cashing in our receipts" with Him, and what that phrase could mean to me when I needed God's help the most.

Matthew 6:10 KJV says *in earth, as it is in heaven.*
God does things on earth the same way as He does
them in heaven. And according to Hebrews 13:8, He
is the same–He changes not. So what He does and
how He operates in heaven is the same unit of measurement He uses here on earth. If we want to find
out what His standards of operation are, just read the
Book...the Bible. It's consistent through and
through.

Matthew 6:33 NJKV says, *"Seek first the kingdom of
God and His righteousness."*
It actually means seek first
the kingdom of God and
His ways of doing and

**God does things on earth
the same way as
He does them in heaven.**

being–then all these things will be added unto you.
Well then, what is the kingdom of God and His way
of doing things? Matthew 13:31-32 says that "the
kingdom of heaven is as a seed, and when it is sown,
it grows up and shoots out." So we learn a principle
here–a very important divine way of how God operates in His kingdom. We first seek His kingdom and
do it that way. The way is simple: The kingdom of
God is equivalent to a seed, and the seed must be
sown, and then it grows.

1. Seek first the kingdom of God.

2. The kingdom of God works on the principle of seed.

3. The seed must be sown to produce a harvest.

God was teaching me His divine mathematics: When you sow, it's multiplied, and it yields a greater harvest for you to reap—to receive. Just as a tiny acorn becomes a mighty oak after it's sown, every seed we sow into the kingdom of God has the potential for a great harvest of return, not only for our benefit, but to spread His Gospel to all the world. As Genesis 12:2 says, "I'll bless you and then make you a blessing."

I remember Mr. Beale, my first banker in Tulsa, and the enormous influence he had in giving me a practical demonstration of God's financial laws in the secular world. This was when I was first coming into sowing and reaping—giving and *receiving*—in 1947. The Lord brought him across my path at the right time to help me better understand the *revelation* which God inspired me to call *Seed-Faith*. That understanding, I believe, has had a unique and positive impact on the body of Christ throughout the world.

I'll never forget the day Mr. Beale sat me down in his office and said, "Reverend Roberts, I have a story I want to tell you that I believe might help you in your life and ministry."

He went on to tell me that one winter he was returning from a bank meeting in another city when his car had a flat tire. It was late at night and very cold. As he got out to fix the flat, he discovered that he didn't know how to use the tire jack or remove the wheel. Before too long, he realized that during his struggle, the temperature had gotten so cold that he was almost at the point of freezing. By then it was midnight, and he didn't know what to do. He tried to flag down other cars, but to his dismay, no one stopped.

So he got back in his car and turned up the heater. He soon realized he was dangerously stranded and his life could be in serious trouble. But almost out of nowhere, a big 18-wheeler drove up, came right to where he was, and stopped. The driver got out and said, "Mister, are you in trouble?"

Mr. Beale said, "Yes, I am," and when he told him his problem, the driver said, "I can fix your flat in 10 minutes. You just get in the car and wait." And just as he said, in about ten minutes he came to let Mr. Beale know the tire was fixed.

When he finished, Mr. Beale offered to pay him. Amazingly he replied, "Oh, no, that was my good deed for the day."

Mr. Beale said, "Wait just a minute." He pulled out his notebook and

I got a true revelation about the power of a receipt.

wrote him a receipt for $200. As he handed it to him, he said, "You don't know me, but I'm a banker. If you ever have need for $200, you just bring this into my bank in Tulsa. You'll find this amount deposited in your account."

As you can imagine, I got a true revelation about the power of a receipt. I thanked Mr. Beale for sharing this story with me about the receipt and the account that was put in the man's name in his bank. I was about to end the conversation when Mr. Beale stopped me and said, "Oh, wait a minute, that is not all," and he proceeded to tell me the best part of the story.

The receipt is a wonderful thing to think about if you ever need it, but the real power of the story is not in the receipt itself—it's when you cash it in.

How *nice* it is to have a piece of paper that says you have money in an account if you ever get desperate. But, oh, what a *huge* difference it is in having that nice piece of paper in times of need, and you can get the *actual* money to pay the bill.

God tells us we have a heavenly account, according to Philippians 4:17.

Mr. Beale said, "The story continues. A few months later, as I was coming out of my office, I heard a discussion between one of my cashiers and a man I recognized as the trucker who had helped me, and possibly saved my life.

"The cashier had the receipt I had signed for the man. She asked him if he had an account in this bank. He replied, 'All I know is that the president of your bank signed this receipt for me, and said if I ever needed $200, to come to this bank and cash it.'

"Immediately, I jumped into the conversation to honor my word to this trucker. I said to the cashier, 'Mrs. Jones, that's my signature on that receipt. He has an account with me, and I personally put the $200 in his account, so please give him the money.'

14

She smiled and handed him two brand-new $100 bills."

Mr. Beale went on to say, "Oral, I just hope you can use this story in your ministry." I thanked him and said, "This has come at a good time in my life." And it had.

That day, I learned a very valuable lesson about seed and harvest, and holding on to a *receipt* that is honored by the most available power behind it. Immediately, I thought of Philippians 4:13-19. This is the story of God telling us He honors every word He said, even in the secular world. God tells us we have a heavenly account, according to verse 17 KJV: *Not because I desire a gift: but I desire fruit* [or resources or provision] *that may abound to your account.*

I've told this story many times. Still, it continues to remind me that each time I give, God Himself is writing out my *receipt* on the "bank" He heads in heaven. It's directly connected on earth to my Christian walk with God—and it's connected to every one of us, as we give to God.

I know transactions like this are going on constantly between those who are operating in God's divine system of *giving* and *receipting* according to His

Word.

I believe that right now you can start a new life with God meeting your needs and challenges that may not otherwise be met. And I believe this principle can be applied in every area of your life, beginning at this moment.

IMPORTANT POINTS TO REMEMBER

1. The trucker had a habit of doing good deeds, not realizing that each was a seed he was planting. One wealthier than he knew a receipt was due him.

2. At a time of need, the trucker knew he could cash in his receipt...and he did.

3. Even in the secular world, sowing and *reaping*–giving and *receiving*–is the chief ingredient of life. This stems from a spiritual principle, and therefore, God is required to honor it.

CHAPTER TWO

My Agreement With Evelyn: "Honey, Let's Cash In Our Receipt With God"

The whole Bible principle of *cashing in your receipt with God*, based on giving and receipting, came alive in me one afternoon in midsummer several years ago. I came in from the golf course, telling Evelyn that I was cramping so badly in my stomach that I could hardly stand up straight.

She said, "Honey, what did you eat on the golf course?"

I replied, "Just an apple."

"Well," Evelyn said, "sometimes an apple cramps my stomach if I don't have other food with it. Let's just pray and ask God to take the cramping away."

So we prayed and believed God for a healing.

She told me to sit down and get quiet while she fixed dinner. She believed when I ate, it would help the extremely severe cramping.

After dinner, I told Evelyn I was still cramping unusually bad. She called our doctor and told him that I was cramping so badly, I could hardly stand the pain.

He asked, "Which side is cramping?" and she told him the right side. He said, "Let me talk to Oral."

So she gave me the phone, and the doctor asked me to tell him exactly where I hurt. I told him, and he said, "Oral, you have appendicitis."

I said, "Doctor, old people don't have appendicitis."

The doctor said, "Oh, yes, they do, and so do little children. Let me talk to Evelyn."

So Evelyn took the phone. The doctor insisted that I had appendicitis and was to be taken to the emergency room immediately, where he would meet us with a surgeon. He insisted we should be prepared to operate that night, or the appendix might burst.

We got into the car and started to the hospital. Both of us were silent, praying and believing God to heal me, when I said, "Evelyn, we've planted a lot of seeds of faith into the Gospel and into the lives of other people. And you know we have *receipts in* heaven that we can cash in. Philippians 4:17 KJV says when the Christian believers gave to Paul, he said, *Not because I desire a gift: but I desire fruit that may abound to your account.*

The doctor insisted that I had appendicitis and was to be taken to the emergency room immediately.

Immediately, Evelyn remembered the concept of sowing and reaping and said, "Yes."

So I said, "According to Matthew 18:19, I want you to agree with me in the Spirit, in the way God set it up in His Word. I want you to agree with me that as I am *cashing in a receipt* tonight for my healing, I'm believing that I won't have to have surgery."

She immediately said, "Yes, honey, I'll agree with you. I don't want you to have to have surgery either." So we held hands and prayed, believing God would relieve the pain and heal the problem.

When we arrived at the emergency room, they had already received a call from our doctor and had the gurney ready. By this time, I was shaking all over with pain. While the nurses worked at taking my temperature, blood pressure, and blood samples, Evelyn said to them, "Can't you give Oral something for the pain?"

Unfortunately, they said, "No, not until the doctor examines him and we get an X-ray."

But soon the doctor came and examined me. He said, "Show me exactly where the pain is." When I showed him, he said, "Yes, you have appendicitis. The surgeon is on the way!" And that was it...*or so it seemed*!

> '*Lord, I'm believing You will intercede, and there will be no surgery.*'

Soon the surgeon walked in. He said, "Oral, show me where you hurt." When I put my finger on the spot, he said, "Yes, it's appendicitis. We must operate tonight. But first I want to get an ultrasound to see what's going on in there."

They put me on the gurney, and the orderly rolled me to the ultrasound room. Evelyn stayed there where the gurney had been, praying, "Jesus, remember we agreed that we would cash in a receipt tonight? I know Seed-Faith living works. We've lived by this principle for years. Lord, I'm believing You will intercede, and there will be no surgery."

In the meantime, in the ultrasound room the radiologist turned on the machine and turned the monitor toward me. The doctor and technicians said, "Yes, there it is, Oral. Your appendix is enlarged and inflamed. You must have surgery tonight."

Now I've had surgery before. God has healed me through surgery. I had no fear of surgery, but this was different. This time, I believe God spoke to me concerning *cashing in a receipt.* This time, I believed I was not supposed to have surgery, and that my healing was to take place differently. Evelyn and I truly believed that I was not supposed to have surgery because of what God had said.

I turned my head toward the wall. With tears streaming down my cheeks, I prayed, "Lord, remember Evelyn and I agreed in the Spirit there would be no surgery? We've planted our seed, we've released our faith, and we're calling in a receipt."

Well, about that time the ultrasound technician said, "Doctor, look!"

The doctor said, "What's happening?"

"There's a cloud coming over the screen. Can you see that, Doctor?"

At that very moment, the pain left my side.

The doctor said, "I don't know what happened, Oral, but the appendicitis is gone. You don't have it anymore. I can't explain this, but I'm watching it as it happens on the screen."

I smiled a big smile at both men. Then, not knowing what else to do with me, the surgeon said, "Well, we usually have the orderly wheel the patient back, but I'm going to do it myself."

As we left the room, the radiologist said, "Well, Doctor, you won't get to use a knife on this man tonight."

So picture this: I was in a wheelchair, not in surgery. The surgeon was pushing the wheelchair, and Evelyn looked up and saw us coming. She was a bit perplexed. She got up out of her chair and said, "Doctor, what happened?"

He said, "I don't know, but his pain is gone. When he came in, he *had* appendicitis—it showed up on the ultrasound screen. But he doesn't have it anymore."

Instantly—in typical Evelyn fashion—she said, "I know, Doctor. I know what happened. God healed him! What do we do now?"

Everybody knows it takes lots of paper signing and sometimes hours to be released from the hospital. But the surgeon looked at her and said, "Just take him home the same way you brought him in."

> **'I know what happened. God healed him!'**

That night, I experienced firsthand the true Bible meaning of *giving* and *receiving* and *cashing in a receipt* with God for a miracle. I immediately reflected on the banker and the story of the receipt he gave that young trucker. And just as that young man had gone to the bank and cashed in on his bank account, I had experienced what it means to go to my heavenly account where, as Paul said in Philippians 4:17, fruit may abound—or be added—to that account.

Like that young trucker, I cashed in my *receipt* on heaven's account, and my heavenly Father honored His Word to me, just as the banker honored his word to that trucker. And imagine: If a banker delighted in honoring his word to a trucker, how much more does God delight in honoring His Word to His children? And doesn't Psalm 35:27 say that God delights in the prosperity—increase in every way—of His children?

That experience greatly increased the different ways I expected to receive the healing power of God into my body. In fact, having shared this with many others since has brought a radical new expectation, inspiring others to expect miracles to happen through their own Seed-Faith giving.

So I want to encourage you to take this revelation to heart and consider making it personal in your own life.

IMPORTANT POINTS TO REMEMBER

1. It's important to keep contact with your physician.

2. It's important to have sown seed in order to cash in your receipt.

3. Use the prayer of agreement.

4. Even when under medical examination or treatment, keep your faith in action.

5. Cashing in your *receipt* works in all areas of your life.

CHAPTER THREE

Learning That Giving Is Not an End in Itself—You Have to Have an Account With the Department of Giving and Receiving

'VE discovered that most believers who give to God are almost totally unaware that each time we give to the Lord, He is holding out a receipt which is based on a personal account we have with Him in His "department of giving and receiving." Or, as the Lord directed me to say it in a more thought-provoking way, in His department of giving and *receipting*. The word *receipt* is defined as "a written acknowledgment of the receiving of goods or money."

It's one thing to put money in an account, but it's totally another thing to have a careful calculation of that money and that account. What if you constantly put money in an account somewhere, but no one kept track, no one kept record of that account? Then when you needed it the most, no one knew where it was, or how much it was, or knew quite what to do about it. Well, according to the Scripture in

I had to work to get into a mindset of being a receiver.

Philippians 4:13-19, that is certainly not the case, for God is very aware of your account. He keeps perfect record of your giving. He holds a perfect receipt for you, and He knows *exactly* what to do when you need to cash it in.

Through my personal experience of over 50 years of sowing and reaping—giving to God of my finances and in all other areas of my life—came a great and powerful revelation from the Word of God. I realized that I was establishing an account, a personal account with God. I simply hadn't been taught that in my Christian life, and therefore, I didn't know that giving is irrevocably connected to receiving—just as sowing is irrevocably connected to reaping a harvest—for with God, one cannot be separated from the other.

In fact, in Genesis 8:22 God specifically said as long as the earth remains, there *shall* be—yes, *shall* be—day and night, hot and cold, winter and spring, seedtime and harvest. No matter how you try to separate day from becoming night, you can't—*one follows the other.* Winter follows spring, cold weather becomes hot, and seedtime turns into a harvest. It is the natural system of progression that God set up, and He is not about to change His system. *I am the Lord, I change not,* says Malachi 3:6 KJV. [I am] *the same yesterday, today, and forever,* we're told in Hebrews 13:8 NKJV.

God set up the system. It works with or without us. We cannot change His system. However, we can miss out on His blessings when we fail to operate within His system. Just because we don't partake of it, doesn't mean it doesn't work. It's God's system, whether we join in or not.

It's a lot like a merry-go-round—it's there, going around all along; whether we jump on it or not, it's still going around. However, it's up to us to get on it and ride and become part of it. The merry-go-round is not going to move; it's not going to change.

I vividly remember the time and place that I received God's revelation to me: that in giving to Him, I was not just giving away my gifts and having less after my giving, but that I would receive back more than I had before. I realized that it was the very same principle as a seed sown in the soil of the earth, which grows into a far larger harvest that is returned to the sower.

That eye-opening revelation by the Holy Spirit from the Word of God—from the teachings of the Lord Jesus, the writings of the apostle Paul, and from others throughout the Bible—*changed my life forever.* Suddenly, I began the journey to turn my Christian giving and believing around. After realizing that wrong teaching and my own failure to understand that giving—even as a faithful tither—was *not an end in itself,* I had to work to get into a mindset of being a *receiver.* It was a new revelation, and I needed to get a clear, biblical understanding of this information.

This was the eternal principle of giving *and receiving,* and I should look *directly to God as my Source of total supply!* The Scripture in 2 Corinthians 9:7 NKJV that says, *God loves a **cheerful** giver,* became a *rhema* word of revelation to me. I mean, I got it! I could give cheerfully and joyfully with full assurance that God, being *a rewarder of those who diligently seek Him* (Hebrews 11:6 NKJV), will reward me according to His Word and my faithfulness in giving according to His system.

> **I woke up to the awareness that every gift I made to God's kingdom, or when I was doing His work, automatically became a receipt.**

Therefore, the joy hit me like a thunderbolt, and I got it.

I woke up to the awareness that every gift I made to God's kingdom, or when I was doing His work, automatically became a receipt, and God personally was laying up and overseeing Oral Roberts' account in heaven. He was multiplying my gifts back toward me constantly, according to my faith, and I could cash in my *receipts* in every area of my life, including my finances, my health...my everything. A light turned on inside me, and for the first time, *I began to see God as He really is.* It was the beginning of my seeing the "whole man" concept that Jesus taught.

In this message from the Word of God, my own personal experience, and from experiences of others who consequently learned it, I want to teach you the possibility of obtaining the God-ordained harvest attached to every seed you sow. I believe you can stop the losses that all too often flow out of your own personal account, leaving you disappointed and weakened in your faith and ability to trust God.

With every seed you sow to God as the Source of your total supply (Philippians 4:19), it is your Bible right to lay hold of Jesus' words in Luke 6:38 and say, "With what measure you give, it shall be measured to you again."

I call this living the Seed-Faith life, not just once in a while in a need or a crisis, but as your way of life on this earth.

IMPORTANT POINTS TO REMEMBER

1. Our life in Christ depends on doing things according to God's Word.
>—My future life changed upon learning that Bible principle.

2. I had to learn giving is *not an end in itself!*
>—I learned every seed I sowed had a receipt on the end of it.

3. Seed-Faith giving and Bible-based receiving is the key to the success of every follower of Jesus Christ.
>—The key Scripture is Philippians 4:15-19. I encourage you to read it out loud often.

4. Cross-check Seed-Faith Scriptures such as:
- Genesis 8:22
- Matthew 17:20
- Luke 10:2
- Luke 13:18,19
- Galatians 6:7,9

>—Study where God calls His Son Jesus the "seed of David."
- Romans 1:3
- 2 Timothy 2:8
- 1 Peter 1:23

5. Remember how God gave me the revelation that **God is a good God,** and that He is the rewarder of those who diligently seek Him (Hebrews 11:6), which means life to every one of us.
>—Allow this principle to begin to change your perspective.

CHAPTER FOUR

One of the Greatest Moments of My Life— Discovering That God Would Meet All My Needs for All My Life

St. Paul's favorite partner family were the believers in the church at Philippi. According to the book of Philippians, each one had caught on to his teaching on *giving and receiving*—or *giving and receipting*—better than any other group of believers in the early church. Although they were already giving to God's work, we get the feeling that they thought they were not "supposed" to receive. Therefore, they failed to *know* they

37

had a receipt in their "account" with God in heaven. They had not caught on to the Bible concept that through their individual faith, they could "cash in" on their account in every type of need.

However, through Paul's clear and repeated teaching on *giving and receiving*, the Philippian Christian brothers and sisters were now catching on to the Seed-Faith life. They were learning the joy of how to *receive back* on a regular basis. They were excited about their receipts, according to

> **A knowing came into my spirit that I could change from giving for giving's sake to giving into an account with God, an account that I could tap into in my times of need.**

God's resources in heaven. It added "spice" to their everyday living that many believers hadn't experienced yet in the early church. It was to this group of believers that Paul first wrote, *And my God shall supply all your need according to His riches in glory by Christ Jesus* (Philippians 4:19 NKJV).

All of us who look to this marvelous Scripture to build up our expectancy to trust God to supply all our needs, do so because the Philippian Christians first opened up this "treasure trove." They were the

38

first to get all their needs met according to the riches in heaven by Christ Jesus. That inspires me to the core of my being.

A **knowing** came into my spirit that I could change from *giving for giving's sake* to *giving into an account with God,* an account that I could tap into in my times of need by the receipts I was accumulating through my new Seed-Faith life.

This was the beginning of a total turnaround in the way God began to meet my needs. What I did in this new understanding of Seed-Faith giving and receiving was *the key* to my future success as a follower of Jesus Christ, in a new and continuous empowerment of my life and ministry.

Looking again at Philippians 4:13-19, notice that it was *only* to this select group of giving and receiving believers that he spoke this to. It wasn't to the general public, or even to every church Paul had attended. These words were reserved for the faithful few who not only understood giving and receiving, but *acted* on it by their faith.

It was here he also used the word *beloved,* and I believe it was because of a unique relationship Paul had with these believers. There was a unique connection from divine inspiration felt by both sides, both Paul in his work for the Gospel and his "partners" in their effort to support his work. Looking closely at Philippians 4:14—"Nevertheless, you have done well that you were a joint partaker in my distress"—joint partaker means partner or participator.

As Paul went out doing God's work and they supported him, they both jointly received God's blessing on their efforts because they did their part. They each did what God required of them in order to spread the Gospel for God's kingdom to be advanced.

Look carefully at Philippians 4:15-19 KJV (please read this out loud as I so often do):

> Now ye Philippians know also, that in the beginning of the gospel, when I departed from Macedonia, no church communicated with me as concerning giving and receiving, but ye only. For even in Thessalonica ye sent once and again unto my necessity. Not because I desire a gift: but I desire fruit that may abound to your account. But I have all, and abound: I am full, having received

of Epaphroditus the things which were sent from you, an odour of a sweet smell, a sacrifice acceptable, well-pleasing to God. But my God shall supply all your need according to his riches in glory by Christ Jesus.

Now go to verse 13 NKJV, that great verse which states, *I can do all things through Christ who strengthens me.* It is our Savior who established the power to give us strength to do all things through this concept of *giving to God and receiving a harvest back* from a well-calculated heavenly account based on the very riches—the total supply—of heaven. These are strong, powerful words establishing the Bible way for our harvesting miracles, based on sowing our faith as a seed unto God and His work. God carefully selected the apostle Paul to instruct us to establish a "Covenant of Blessing" with God that dates all the way back to the blessing of Abraham established in Genesis 22.

> **God carefully selected the apostle Paul to instruct us to establish a 'Covenant of Blessing' with God that dates all the way back to the blessing of Abraham.**

I remember when I first discovered this Scripture

in Philippians 4. It seemed to ignite in my spirit, and I stopped and reread it several times nonstop. And I've continued to read and meditate on it. It immediately showed me that my giving was a seed of my faith which was directly connected to the harvest through the eternal principle Paul calls sowing and reaping in Galatians 6:7. Here I was learning that Paul is *connecting* our *financial* giving and our *financial receiving.* He explains the scriptural purpose and use of money, and that all our financial needs may be met from a higher Source, rather than being restricted to a limited earthly origin.

> **Each time we sow, we are to look directly to God, our Source, to receive a continuous miracle harvest back as we continue cashing in our receipts.**

This is why each time we sow, we are to look directly to *God, our Source,* to receive a continuous miracle harvest back as we continue cashing in our receipts. This is to be personal to us, something we can see and touch and make full use of as we face the devil's attacks on us throughout the constant demands of life.

I well remember how, as a young preacher, I

dreaded to talk about money, for fear if I did, Christians would think it meant that all I thought about was money. So in my preaching, I didn't face up to the real needs of myself, my wife and children, and my congregation. I have apologized many times for not teaching the people of the churches I pastored that *receiving follows giving, reaping follows seeding*, that *giving carries a receipt* on God's supply...and that we are to place equal emphasis on both giving and receiving.

This is an all-important principle of the Word of God, with the understanding that giving and receipting always work together for us. That's the way God meets our needs. I can testify that this principle changed my entire perspective on scriptural prosperity and giving and receiving in my life when I embraced it with my whole being.

Paul certainly didn't separate giving and receiving in his teachings, and God strongly dealt with me to boldly teach and preach this Seed-Faith message to His people.

So I began a most unusual journey of instruction on this most important scriptural principle. Not only must you give to receive back, but you must constantly *expect* to receive back from God, your Source. What you sow away from yourself sets you in position to expect a miracle harvest—because this is God's way of operating, according to the Bible.

As a result, I confronted people with a scriptural principle as completely new to them as it had been to me. So from that time on, every time I have referred to giving, I have tied it with *receiving*, just as Paul did in Philippians 4:15, *giving and receiving* and *sowing and reaping*, as he did in Galatians 6:7.

I have told everyone, that as for me, when I learned to give, *I made a choice* at that moment to begin thinking of receiving back from God and not any person, but directly from the "Account Holder" in heaven—God, who is the "Lord of the harvest" (Luke 10:2), as well as the "Lord of the seed" (Luke 13:18-19). They both are part of the same truth of God and of His purpose for meeting the needs that occupy such an important and necessary place in our lives, and above all, in carrying out the work of God throughout the earth.

Most of the spiritual leaders I came up under seemed to think money was all right for the people of the world to have, but was not to be expected by the

people of God. All I had heard from them was that
we were to give, even to tithe, but we were not to
expect anything back, not even from God. But now
there was a radical change in me, and I began teaching that God is against the *poverty mentality*, and He
desires "all our needs to
be met" (Philippians
4:19). Not part of our
needs…not just for our
souls to be saved by the
blood of Jesus…but our

> *I began teaching that God is against the poverty mentality, and He desires 'all our needs to be met.'*

financial needs, our health needs, our family needs;
in fact, *all our needs.*

What was previously communicated was a gospel
of "God, You keep Oral Roberts humble, and we'll
keep him poor." And that's the way I lived the first
12 years of my Christian life and ministry. I was terribly frustrated at not being able to meet the needs of
my wife and children. I was terribly embarrassed at
the grocery store when there were times Evelyn filled
her basket and was going to pay, but she didn't have
enough money and had to return several items back
to the shelves. When she told me of these times, she
hurt so bad that she was in tears. It made me angry

at God, and at myself as the father of the family. This hurt my faith and peace of mind and sense of responsibility.

I worked so hard, but it seemed something bad was happening to me because I was called to the ministry. Just because I loved God and worked hard was no reason my family had to suffer and not have food and the things we desperately needed. I hated it! Worst of all, I didn't know the way out

> **I saw that His highest wish was that 'I prosper and be in health even at the same level that my soul prospers.'**

of this mess I was in. I found no one I could talk to.

It was a great day when God took my blindness away and I began to see that if I gave my best to God, I could ask Him for His best in return—and if I expected it and did not give up in my expectation, *my miracle return* would not pass me by. Galatians 6:9 KJV brought me great strength: *And let us not be weary in well doing: for in due season we shall reap, if we faint not.*

One of the best things in looking to God as the Source of my total supply was the fact that my miracle return would not be limited to man's provision.

It would be returned to me based on a *much higher measurement*—a higher authority. Amazingly, I learned it would be according to *his riches in glory by Christ Jesus*, as Philippians 4:19 KJV explicitly declares.

Getting this new concept into my life changed my giving into *a new expectation* that I would be assured to receive. I could cash in my receipts. Great peace came into my heart and a new boldness to trust God. It was not just with my mouth, but with new *knowledge* and a *knowing* in my heart that my Savior truly wanted to supply my every need, that He actually wanted to bless and prosper me. I saw that His highest wish was that "I prosper and be in health even at the same level that my soul prospers" (3 John 2).

And then it hit me like a clap of thunder. In a flash I got it: I saw that He wanted each of us to live in His *reward system* (Hebrews 11:6).

I saw Him as a good God who wanted all good for His people, who wanted to make them totally different from all people: prosperous, happy, and joyous sons and daughters of His. For the first time, I saw that in spite of hardships, persecutions, sufferings, and bad things coming at us all through our Christian walk, we can live a victorious life.

Isaiah 54:17 says "no weapon formed against us shall prosper." It doesn't mean that there won't be anything that comes against us. It means that whatever satan throws against us can be overcome by the power of our faith in God. And that was what I wanted most: to live a victorious life of faith in Christ all the days of my life. I knew the Bible teaching that "the just shall live by faith" (Habakkuk 2:4; Romans 1:17; Galatians 3:11; Hebrews 10:38), and I was finally finding the Bible principle of *doing* it.

Out of this new beginning in my life leaped the revelation that **God is a good God**, a *rhema* word, fresh and new to me at that time in May 1947. And as unusual and different to people as it was in 1947, it has since opened the eyes of people all over the world to the fact that God is indeed a **good God**. I never get tired of saying it. It means life to me—and life to everyone who believes God's goodness and that "He is a rewarder of them who diligently seek him" (Hebrews 11:6), which enables us to "cash in our receipts."

IMPORTANT POINTS TO REMEMBER

1. Remember, the apostle Paul clearly and repeatedly taught the eternal principle of **giving and receiving.**

—It's very important to read and re-read Philippians 4:15-19.

2. It's most important to know God has a way for you to get *all your needs met,* according to His reward system of His riches in glory by Christ Jesus.

3. We must do what Paul did when he connected giving and receipting and did not separate the two.

4. You *can make a choice* that you can live a prosperous, victorious life in Christ at the same level as your soul prospers (3 John 2).

—Truly God is a good God.

CHAPTER FIVE

Let's Take a Closer Look at the Other Bible Word for Receiving, Which Is *Receipting*

I n Philippians 4:15 KJV Paul says to his fellow brothers and sisters in Christ, *Now...concerning giving and receiving....* I'm told in the original Greek language—the language in which Paul wrote his books in the New Testament—the translators into English could just as well have used the word *receipting*, as the word *receiving*.

I do not know why they chose *receiving* instead of *receipting* except maybe r-e-c-e-i-v-i-n-g at that time in history might have been understood better than r-e-c-e-i-p-t-i-n-g.

But since the entire context of the text was about an account and God's heavenly record-keeping of that account, the word *receipting* gives us a better understanding of what was taking place in the heavenlies.

When we go to a bank and put something in, we get a receipt to have a record of that transaction, so that when the time comes to make a withdrawal on the account and receive back what's rightfully ours, the receiving is accurate and fair.

Upon further study, I saw they could have used the word *receipting* because of Paul's next words: *For even in Thessalonica ye sent once and again unto my necessity. Not because I desire a gift: but I desire fruit that may abound to your account* (Philippians 4:16-17 KJV).

These believers were "again and again" givers, consistent in their giving and receiving (receipting). You see, each time the seed of their faith was "deposited" into their account, a receipt in heaven was necessary. Then, accurate return on receiving could take place. *And for what purpose?* Paul explains: "Not that I desire a gift, but I desire fruit (results) that may abound (overflow) to your account (with God)" —*so that God may give back to you*!

Paul was not writing about a personal get-rich scheme. A thousand times NO! And don't think for a minute that God doesn't judge the heart. As Galatians 6:7 KJV says, *Be not deceived; God is not mocked: for whatsoever a man soweth, that shall he also reap.* Of course, through his own *giving* and *receiving* (*receipting*), Paul expected his own needs to be met, as we'll see in the next verses.

> **These believers were 'again and again' givers, consistent in their giving and receiving (receipting).**

I remember asking the question, Why couldn't the translators have used the word *receipting* equally as well as *receiving*? I quickly saw that Paul was giving the good results—from a good God—by explaining, "Not that I desire a gift, but I desire fruit may abound to *your account*." When you give, you have an account with God, make no mistake about it.

Paul *knew* his teachings would be misunderstood, and he immediately explained it to put a stop to the wrong interpretation of his motives. Satan would love to use these wrong motives to trip up believers and convince them to miss their blessing by missing out on sowing. So to avoid that, Paul immediately made reference to be careful and not get into wrong thinking here.

In other words, with each act of giving, a deposit is being made to a believer's heavenly account. And with an account on deposit in heaven's bank, I can cash in my receipts according to my need in both spiritual *and* earthly—or material—form. I remember saying to myself, *Wow! Talk about opening my mind and the joy of the Lord filling my heart!*

When you give, you have an account with God, make no mistake about it.

From that hour, I began thinking of giving and *receiving* equally with giving and *receipting*. This has continued to happen to me without fail for these uninterrupted 59 years of my ministry and in my personal life and family. It is thrilling to see hundreds of others have now grasped the meaning of the Bible teaching of the Seed-Faith life. The happy changes brought about are thrusting us into a deeper dimension of service to God.

IMPORTANT POINTS TO REMEMBER

1. Look at the other word for receiving: *receipting*
   —Philippians 4:16-17
   —The Bible translators could just have easily
   interchanged the word *receiving* with *receipting*
   to show God's accurate record-keeping in our
   heavenly account for the cashing in of our receipts.

2. Remember in our giving, deposits are being kept
record of by the "Master Banker" to our account
(Philippians 4:16-17).
   —As a giver from the beginning of my Christian life,
   I did not know I had a receipt with God.
   —Wrong teaching robs God's people. Right
   teaching reaps the benefits God Himself
   establishes and wants us to have, according to
   His riches in glory by His Son Christ Jesus.
   It is the one sure way to live by faith, which is how
   God does things, and we are to follow His example.

CHAPTER SIX

The Amazing Change in My Life When I Stopped Being Afraid of God

The night of my conversion, while I lay deathly ill with tuberculosis, I was only 17 years old. I had a Cherokee Indian mother, and in those days, many Cherokee Indians in Oklahoma suffered early deaths from tuberculosis. In fact, my mother's father and two of her older sisters had died from TB.

After collapsing in the final game of the southern Oklahoma basketball tournament—while dribbling toward the jump shot that would win the game—I began hemorrhaging from my lungs. As blood began running from my mouth, I literally felt life going out of my lungs. I was carried home and given the news that I, too, was dying from tuberculosis.

Week after week, I lay in bed, coughing and spitting up blood, sometimes so violently that the walls were spattered with it. I ate almost nothing except the raw eggs and milk that were often prescribed for tuberculosis in those days. I continued to lose weight and grow weaker, until those who visited me were shocked by my emaciated appearance.

> *Every dream I'd ever had was swept away, along with any possibility of getting well.*

Although I had wonderful doctors, they gave my parents no medical hope that I would recover. Eventually, arrangements were made for me to be admitted to the state TB hospital in Talihina, Oklahoma, in the midst of the Cherokee Indian Nation. It was as if my life was over before it had really begun. Every dream I'd ever had was swept away, along with any possibility of getting well.

For months, people prayed for me, and the doctors did what they could do for me, but nothing seemed to help. My brother Vaden—who I was especially close to—broke down in tears at my bedside one day and said, "God, take this away from Oral and give it to me. I'm stronger and older than he is. Maybe I can take it better." My heart was so touched. I saw so much love in Vaden, but I had a hard time believing God could love me.

So many people kept telling my parents, "God put this on Oral. God is punishing Oral." I was only 17—what could I possibly have done for God to hate me so much that He would put this on me? that He would do this to me?

You see, I grew up under that "gospel" of a God who punishes and a God who expects poverty to be equal to humility, and that the poorer and sicker you were, the more you were serving Him. Today I see how completely ridiculous that is and how against the Word of God in His Bible that is, but as the Lord lives, *that's* what we were taught in church! *So surely God could not care about a young man like me*, I thought to myself...not the scary God I had run away from.

But one day, as Papa knelt at the foot of my bed

and began to pray for my salvation, something felt different. I felt a warmth come into my body. I looked up into Papa's face, and as I watched the tears flow from his eyes, his face disappeared from my sight, and in its place I saw the face of Jesus. Whether I saw Jesus with my physical eyes or with the eyes of my spirit, it made no difference to me. In a moment's time, I called on the God of my youth...the God of my parents...the God I had run from, crying, "Save me, Jesus. Save me!" My family began crying, laughing, and praising God all at once, and I was born into the kingdom of God that very hour.

Directly after my salvation experience—and still deathly ill—I thought about the $14 that different friends had given to me during the 163 days of being bedridden and hemorrhaging my life's blood away. All I could think of was asking my mother to bring that money to me. I counted out the tithe, or one-tenth, of that $14 and handed the $1.40 to my pastor father to put into the Lord's work. I remember to this day how excited I was as the tithe left my hand to go into God's hand through His work here on earth. I felt it was the best bargain of my life—I got to exchange my tithe for His blessing according to exactly what He said in Malachi 3:10-11. And I've felt that same way through all the years since that day.

Even as a 17-year-old boy at the point of death—without the slightest idea I would ever preach the Gospel—I can't begin to tell you the thrill I felt when I gave my tenth, my tithe offering, unto God that night. I really got a grasp, a revelation, that I had given to God.

Yet I missed something that night which took 12 years to learn: It was that on the other end of that little $1.40 tithe was the divine *connection* to *receipting*. It was now in

> *Even as a 17-year-old boy at the point of death—without the slightest idea I would ever preach the Gospel—I can't begin to tell you the thrill I felt when I gave my tenth, my tithe offering, unto God that night.*

the hands of Him "who multiplies our seed sown" (Galatians 6:7). At that time, my parents and I were not aware of the Bible principle of seedtime and harvest, which is first described in Genesis 8:22 KJV: *While the earth remaineth, **seedtime and harvest**, and cold and heat, and summer and winter, and day and night shall not cease.* And it continues through

Malachi 3:10-11 KJV:

> Bring ye all the tithes into the store-
> house, that there may be meat in mine
> house, and prove me now here with, saith
> the Lord of hosts, if I
> will not open you the
> windows of heaven,
> and pour you out a
> blessing, that there
> shall not be room
> enough to receive it.
> And I will rebuke
> the devourer for your sakes, and he shall
> not destroy the fruit of your ground;
> neither shall your vine cast her fruit before
> the time in the field, saith the Lord of hosts.

The apostle Paul connected giving and receiving together. At every point he taught on giving, he connected it with seedtime and harvest.

It goes on into Luke 6:38 KJV, where Jesus says, *Give, and it shall be given unto you; good measure, pressed down, and shaken together, and running over, shall men give into your bosom. For with the same measure that ye mete withal it shall be measured to you again.*

And it continues into Galatians 6:7 KJV, *Be not deceived; God is not mocked: for whatsoever a man soweth, that shall he also reap,* and countless other

Scriptures.

By teaching about giving—and stopping there without going on into receiving back the harvest—the church may have missed a great opportunity to fulfill Scriptures and teach God's people how to rely on the Word of God for their final authority on prosperity. Not understanding that making our faith an act of our giving—a seed sown that creates for us a Bible *receipt* that we can cash with God—I believe has created possibly *one of the major blunders* of misunderstanding of God's reward system; and therefore, it has *cheated so many* of God's people of the *untold wealth, health, and prosperity God has stored up for the righteous.*

The apostle Paul connected giving and receiving *together.* At every point he taught on giving, he connected it with seedtime and harvest. In Galatians 6:7 KJV he said, *For whatsoever a man soweth, that shall he also reap.* You *sow* it, God will *grow* it, and you will *reap* it, providing you believe it and set your faith on God who calls Himself the "Lord of the harvest." You must see in your mind and spirit that your harvest must be directly attached to the other end of your seed and your faith.

In Paul's letter to the Philippians, he told them, *No church shared with me concerning **giving and receiving** but you only. For even in Thessalonica you sent aid once and again for my necessities. Not that I seek the gift, **but I seek the fruit that abounds to your account*** (Philippians 4:15-17 NKJV). Paul pointed out that **God pays attention to our giving, immediately making a receipt for it to our account.** Just thinking about my receipts thrills me!

It is my belief that Paul's teaching on giving and receiving came out of his understanding of tithing under the Old Covenant. As he studied Malachi 3:10—after he had come up under the New Covenant—he saw that God had a deeper meaning in having His people give. Their giving *proved* Him, giving evidence of His goodness. Under the risen Christ, Paul was inspired of the Holy Spirit to put all the words of Malachi 3:10 into three words: *giving and receiving* (receipting).

Therefore, the tithes and offerings under the New Covenant of Jesus Christ are given as Seed-Faith, with a knowing that our giving will be multiplied to be received back in a measure *according to* [God's] *riches in glory by Christ Jesus* (Philippians 4:19 KJV).

In Malachi 3:10, God's blessings of return were *uncontainable*. In Philippians 4:19 they are *inexhaustible*. When we act by faith and establish a rhythm of giving and receiving, sowing and reaping, we can experience the joyous and abundant returns that God so loves to give us. It is a vital and living part of God's reward system.

> **You sow it, God will grow it, and you will reap it, providing you believe it and set your faith on God.**

Although I faithfully continued my tithing through my giving for the next 12 years, again and again the spiritual leaders over me, a young minister of the Gospel, continued to preach and teach that we were to give, but with little or no emphasis that we were to expect to receive anything back. "Giving is a totally unselfish act," they taught, *leaving out the clear teaching of the entire Word of God that* **giving and receiving are compared to seedtime and harvest, and they belong together— always**.

God reminded me that Christians do not take a vow of poverty, and this includes ministers of the Gospel. When our bills roll around, the groups or companies we work with do not say, "Oh, don't worry, just working here is a gift to us. You'll be fine. That will pay your bills." Nor is it scriptural—but seedtime and harvest is scriptural.

Bills have to be paid—food, clothing, housing, transportation, education, medical help, and all other necessities of life have to be paid for—or we will do without. If we do without, we fall below the poverty line—and there, in most cases, giving stops, for there's little or nothing to give. If giving stops, immediately receiving stops also. Added to the suffering of the person and the family is to not have the money to do anything except barely exist.

Tithes and offerings under the New Covenant of Jesus Christ are given as Seed-Faith.

No, a thousand times no! Both Jesus and Paul tell us that the workman is worthy of his hire (Luke 10:7), so "muzzle not the ox (the workman) that treadeth out the corn" (1 Corinthians 9:9).

"God delights in the prosperity of His children" (Psalm 35:27), and Haggai 2:8 says that all the gold and silver in the earth was put there by God. God goes on to say in Genesis 1:26 that we are to subdue the earth and take dominion over it.

For 59 years I have lived under what I believe is the very essence, the heart, of the Word of God: *seedtime and harvest, sowing and reaping, giving and receiving (receipting)*. In fact, Matthew 6:33 says we are to seek first the kingdom of God and His ways of doing and being, and the other things we have need of will be added unto us. Jesus explains how we can seek the kingdom of God; in Mark 4:26, He says the kingdom of God is as a seed. Sowing was so important to God that He compared His entire kingdom to a seed that must be sown, a seed that would grow up and produce after whatever kind of seed was sown— good or bad...big or small.

I believe we are under *hire* from God. We are *His* workmen, and each of us believers—including God's ministers of His Gospel—like the oxen, must not be muzzled or stopped from doing the job we are designed to do, and then reaping the harvest from it for our own needs.

Why God chose me, at age 29, to be in the fore-front to help His people begin breaking out of the bondage of terrible needs not being met, I don't know. But it came out of a very real crisis experi-ence, as so many things do, and as a result of enormous poverty. I was just poor enough to ask God what He thought of my family living just above starvation…and what did He intend to do about it?

That resulted in His reply that He had already done something about it—He put all the gold and silver in the earth (Haggai 2:8), and He told us to take dominion over it (Genesis 1:26). He delights in our prosperity (Psalm 35:27). He gave us *power* to get wealth (Deuteronomy 8:18). He wishes above all things that we prosper and be in health, even as our soul prospers (3 John 2). He sent Jesus to the Cross to save, heal, and deliver us in every area of our lives. The only thing left to do is for *us*, as believers, to go ahead and receive it as part of our Christian heritage.

IMPORTANT POINTS TO REMEMBER

1. When I had a genuine new-birth experience, which led to my healing from tuberculosis, it changed everything for me.

> —Jesus promised that upon receiving Him into our hearts and lives, old things would go by the wayside, and in Christ we could declare that all things become new (2 Corinthians 5:17).

2. My first time giving was extremely small, but it was a beginning, and little is much when God is in it.

3. I have bad memories of the first 12 years of my ministry.

> —This was before I understood from God's Word that I was under *hire* from the Lord. Then I learned we are worthy of our hire, and God is fair and just.

4. Our lives are not limited by the dollars on our paychecks; our lives are subject to God's unlimited resources (Malachi 3:10-11 and Philippians 4:19).

> —He wants to meet *all our needs*—not just part of them—according to a measurement based on giving and receiving, sowing and reaping, of making our faith a seed that we sow, and looking to Him as our Source.

CHAPTER SEVEN

The Remarkable Wheat Farmer Who Taught Me That Giving Is a Seed

In 1947, I was pastoring a church that had no parsonage for their pastor. I had no money with which to rent or buy even a tiny place for my family. Evelyn and our children and I were taken in temporarily by a couple and their family into their little house. Although we owe them a debt for their sacrifice, it was a very crowded condition. Not only did it put a strain on our family, it really put a strain on their family as well, and I must admit that was hard on me as the provider.

It was bad enough that my family was suffering, but because of my poverty lifestyle and poverty mentality, I was messing up my family and this family as well.

Meanwhile, I was trying to prevail upon the church to purchase a parsonage, not only for while I was their pastor, but for pastors who would follow. For whatever reason, I couldn't break through.

I knew I was called by God to pastor—but definitely not called by Him to starve myself and my family in the process—so I was obviously in a mess.

Our staying with this giving family was reaching a crisis point. Two families—four adults and five children—in a little two-bedroom house just wasn't working out. Besides, there were two women trying to raise their families. It was just a failure on my part, as I was not providing for my family. Yet I knew I was called by God to pastor—but definitely not called by Him to starve myself and my family in the process—so I was obviously in a mess.

Evelyn felt for this family. She poured out her heart to me and said, "Oral, if you don't get us a place to live, I'm going to have to take these children to my mother's, and I can't bring them back until you do. It's just not right what we're doing to this family."

"You wouldn't do that, Evelyn!"

"Just watch me."

That shook me up, and at the next Wednesday night prayer meeting service at the church, I was heavily burdened. The church board wouldn't act, and the church people thought I was a great young man for sacrificing (I felt it was more of a demonic contest).

During my sermon, suddenly I felt the Spirit of the Lord moving upon me to ask the church people to help me raise the down payment on a parsonage, and to start it with my week's salary—which I had on my person—from the previous week: the sum of $55.

I stopped and laid this check on the altar and asked the others to give as they felt led of the Lord.

To my happy surprise, in minutes the down payment was placed by my gift—my seed. I went home to tell Evelyn she didn't have to take the children to her mother's.

When I told her I had given our week's salary, she

cried, "How am I going to buy groceries for the children on Saturday?" Well, I was caught between two opinions: Should I or should I not have given?

It was wintertime, and believe me, ours was a cold bed that night.

At 4:00 a.m. we were awakened by a knock on the door. I answered it, and it was Art Newfield, farmer, who was a member of the church, and a large wheat farmer.

"Pastor, forgive me for waking you at this hour," Art said. "I was at the prayer meeting tonight, but didn't give anything for the parsonage.

"I went home, but couldn't sleep. A little while ago I got up, went out in the yard, and dug this up." And he handed me four $100 bills.

I'd never held a hundred-dollar bill in my life. Art said, "Pastor, this is not just money I'm giving; it is seed. As you know, I'm a farmer, and I know I have to plant seed to get a harvest.

"I've been playing the stock market and losing my shirt. I could lose my farm. The only way I know to turn this around is to plant a seed out of my trouble." He asked me to pray for him and he left.

Evelyn was looking around the door, and I went

over and just shook the four $100 bills in her face.

"Think of it, darling! I gave our $55 and the Lord has already given us seven times more!"

Talk about being awakened in my spirit and mind—this did it. I'd grown up on a farm the first 14 years of my life, had helped my father in the fields, and understood

> *When I told her I had given our week's salary, she cried, 'How am I going to buy groceries for the children on Saturday?'*

we had to first plant seed to get a crop. But I'd never applied that to my spiritual life before that experience with Art Newfield. It changed my life...forever.

Seed-Faith was born in my heart. It grew and grew, until by my preaching it worldwide, it's become a household word today. There's no way to estimate the millions of people who, through thinking of their giving as a seed they sowed, saw it could be multiplied back many fold, especially *if they were expecting to receive from God as their Source!*

I'll not belabor the point of the opposition I underwent from critics and opposers of *receiving* being *connected* to *giving*. But just ask any "seedfaither," and I think you'll find a happy giver who has learned to receive. I think also you'll realize hundreds of millions of dollars are coming into the kingdom of God, which without Seed-Faith, would not be happening. Most pastors I know, when receiving the tithes and offerings on Sunday morning—or

Talk about being awakened in my spirit and mind—this did it.

who are getting ready to build or add to church property or send forth missionaries—begin by telling the people, "Let's plant our seed and expect God to multiply it back."

Thank God, others have added their scriptural understanding to the Seed-Faith revelation given to me.

Just where are you today in your finances, your money supply, and even more serious needs—including healing—being met?

Do you know the absolute joy of *giving* based on the sure knowledge that it is the Bible foundation for your *receiving*…your seed being multiplied…being able to cash in your receipt with God?

Are you aware that your giving is "not a debt you owe but a seed you sow," with the understanding that if you had all the money in the world, you couldn't buy the miracles of God, because it was Jesus who paid it all? It is through knowing that Jesus Christ is your personal Lord and Savior that you realize God is your Source and you are to expect miracles.

Let's talk about expecting miracle harvests—a new one every day.

IMPORTANT POINTS TO REMEMBER

1. There is a value in learning that what we give is not just money or anything else, but a seed we sow.

—I will always remember Art Newfield and his miracle word to me.

2. Can anyone estimate the abundant finances coming into the spread of the Gospel through making our faith a seed we sow?

—And there's far more to come.

—Yet we can't buy anything from God; Jesus paid it all.

3. Remember: God is your Source.

CHAPTER EIGHT

Cashing In Your Receipt by Expecting a Miracle, and Expecting a New Miracle Every Day

The dynamic phrase, "Expect a miracle, and expect a new miracle every day," came to me at a dangerous time in my life during one of my Miami, Florida, crusades in the mid-fifties.

I had just taken the crusades on national television, and it had created a lot of interest and excitement, both for and against what God was doing in the area of the healing ministry.

Nationally, in the late 1940s, healing had rarely

been experienced by the sick in the United States, and the body of Christ as a whole, and it had certainly not been seen in a public way with large crowds and with such obvious miracles. So as a result, my ministry took on a substantial increase in audiences everywhere I went. Many were traveling across the country to attend and to experience what God was doing through a young, part-Cherokee Indian preacher from Oklahoma. Pastors were flocking to the services, and my invitations to preach were increasing dramatically.

They wanted to kill me...not because well people were getting sick, but because sick people were getting well in Jesus' name.

For some reason very foreign to me, seeing sick people healed didn't set well with the critics in some of the places where we stretched the big tent, or in some of the largest auditoriums in America and some of the stadiums overseas.

Violence erupted like I had never seen before. Attempts were made to take my life by outraged people who were literally sent from the devil, all because sick people were being healed in the name of Jesus, as He commanded us to do in Mark. It amazed me. They wanted to kill me…not because well people were getting sick, but because sick people were getting well in Jesus' name.

Mark 16:17-18 says, "In My name you shall cast out devils, speak with new tongues, lay hands on the sick, and they shall recover." And people wanted to kill me for doing what Jesus told us to do and for believing that the Word of God was true. It completely took me by surprise.

I'll never forget the attempt on my life that came when, without announcement, I allowed precious African-American people to integrate the services, the salvation call, the invalid tent, and the public healing line—and I did it just as God had instructed me to, for it was the cry of His heart.

The chairman of the crusade in a certain city and my associate evangelist, Reverend Robert DeWeese, brought to me the threat from a white supremacist group that said if I didn't publicly segregate the seats in the audience the next night, they would shoot me out of the pulpit.

As a result of these threats, the 25 sponsoring pastors met and left the decision up to me. After meeting with Bob and asking God His opinion, we agreed to leave it how God had said. Being in the ministry of compassion, how could we do any less? We chose to say nothing and let God handle the critics, for it was His service to begin with.

In the midst of all the repeated threats, coming out for the service the next night, I must admit, caused me to approach the platform feeling a little shaky.

Apparently the word had gotten out all over, and along with many others, I felt such a tension in the atmosphere in the tent. But when I read my text, I forgot everything except to preach the Gospel. There were no shots fired and nothing changed. We integrated all services everywhere thereafter, as we have to this day.

Right is right, and if a price has to be paid for it, so be it.

The pastors and my team cooperated with the police and the media, putting guards in place, and the services went on.

At another time, there was a threat in Miami of a different nature, and from my standpoint, more serious. The head of an American group of atheists had told the media they were going to come to the pulpit and make a citizen's arrest of me for praying for the healing of the sick—"practicing medicine without a license."

That afternoon I lay down to take my nap. This was a standard practice I followed to be fresh and rested for the long and compelling night services: preaching, leading hundreds of people to Christ,

Right is right, and if a price has to be paid for it, so be it.

praying for over 100 invalids at each service, and the one-and-a-half to two-hour public healing lines that left me thoroughly physically exhausted.

As I lay across the bed, my body began to tremble. I broke out in a cold sweat. Plainly, I was scared. Illusions of failure for my calling struck my being, and I began feeling defeat in my spirit.

Evidently, my crusades and the films of the services—including the actual healing line with names and addresses of the people I prayed for—were a menace to the beliefs of certain atheistic groups, which they could not allow to continue.

Finally I fell asleep, and when I awakened, God was speaking into my spirit definite words on what I was to do in the service regardless of what else happened.

"Expect a miracle!" He said distinctly to me, a phrase I'd never heard or read before. Then He added, "And expect a new miracle every day!"

As usual, when I experienced the Lord speaking to me, I asked that He repeat the same words three times, which He did, so clearly that there was

> *The phrase, Expect a Miracle, had got hold of me, emptying my mind of every fear.*

no way I could ever doubt them or think that they had come out of my own mind.

When I entered the service that evening, I didn't enter a side door, but the front, walking alone down the long aisle to the platform. I felt a powerful anointing and energizing, my body feeling a little like I was floating.

The phrase, **Expect a Miracle**, had got hold of me, emptying my mind of every fear, and running my cup over with a readiness and boldness to face anything men could do to me.

When I told this to the audience, you could have heard a pin drop—at first.

The media was all over the place, photographers ready to capture the scene of my being led to jail. Instead, when I spoke the Lord's words, *"Expect a miracle, and expect a new miracle every day,"* suddenly it was like a breath whooshing from 10,000 bodies, including mine.

Everything changed in the atmosphere, attitude, and response of the people. **It was the defining moment of my time in church history.**

The phrase spread in the media. Soon it was being picked up everywhere it seemed, and is stronger than ever today.

Never again was I confronted with a citizen's arrest. A lot of fear I didn't realize I had in me left as

Expect a Miracle,

and Expect a New Miracle Every Day

became an integral part of my thoughts, my vocabulary, my writings, and in a large part, of the body of Christ. It can mean a great deal toward helping you *cash in your receipts* far more often.

IMPORTANT POINTS TO REMEMBER

1. Living our convictions may endanger us at times, but it's God's way.

2. Threats have to be faced, but can be faced so much better with a *rhema* word from the Lord.

3. *Expect a miracle, and expect a new miracle every day*—a defining slogan for the body of Christ for our personal lives and witness to the world.
  —A miracle settles the issue.

4. Expecting a miracle is both an attitude and a daily expectancy.

CHAPTER NINE

Consider a Woman Who Simply Wouldn't Say "No" to Cashing In Her Receipt

One night I had finished preaching, giving the invitation to the unsaved, going out to the invalid tent and praying for over 100 sick people, and returning to pray for those who were physically able to enter the public healing line. I had prayed nearly two hours, touching each one in Jesus' name, and after the long service, my energy ran out.

Knowing from long experience that when I grew physically weary, my faith was not as strong, I called a halt and asked the audience to stand for the benediction, stating I would begin the next night where I had ended that service.

I was led to the car to be driven to my hotel room where I would get a strong night's rest to restore my strength.

I took care of myself during the day: refusing all visits and use of my voice, remaining quiet before the Lord, including a nap from 3:00 to 4:00 p.m., eating an easy dinner in my room, and not leaving for the evening service until God's anointing came upon me. Because of this, I was able to have a lot of energy in my body and to appear fresh and strong as I ministered with everything I had until I had preached full sermons, prayed for all invalids who were brought to that service, then prayed personally for several hundreds in the healing line.

It has been amazing to me through the many years of my crusades that I laid hands on and prayed for the healing of approximately 1.5 million sick people.

The Lord did not use me much through the word of knowledge where I could call the sick out of the audience by my voice and have them come to the platform and testify to what God had done in their lives, although today that has become a very effective way the Lord is working.

My calling was to *lay hands on the sick*. This had two effects:

First, it enabled me to identify very personally and individually with the sick person's illness, to feel deep within me what they were feeling. It was also a better way to discern the "measure of faith" they had, as God has revealed He has given to every person. The apostle Paul, no stranger to being a powerful instrument to heal the sick, tells us, "God has given to every man the measure of faith" (Romans 12:3).

It has been amazing to me through the many years of my crusades that I laid hands on and prayed for the healing of approximately 1.5 million sick people, virtually from every walk of life, and suffering from multiple afflictions. Amazing also is the fact that I never caught one of the more infectious diseases, especially in the invalid room.

It seemed as though God knew what I would be doing, and during that period, He blessed me with supernatural strength. For example, for over three hours I was in personal control in every service, preaching, teaching, leading large numbers to receive Christ as their personal Savior, praying for 100 to 200 invalids in each service, and laying hands on literally hundreds until we were nearing midnight. The television cameras caught all this for national television, as we were the first to do this live and be on nearly 200 powerful TV stations each week.

Beginning in 1954, working under the blinding lights each week, bringing the audience the good news that God heals today right into their living rooms...only I knew the tremendous endurance this took and the energy of my being that it consumed. There was no way to explain it to anyone who hadn't gone through it, and yet, God kept me strong in the midst of it. After each crusade, I was thoroughly exhausted. But during them, I was thoroughly exhilarated. It's an experience that has marked my life for time and eternity.

One evening, I announced I was out of strength and would have to close the service. I was hurrying to the car when a woman came up behind me, grabbed the back of my coat, stopped me, and whirled me around toward her. Bursting into tears, she cried, "Oral Roberts, you stopped the healing line too quick. I am very sick and have traveled hundreds of miles by bus to get here. I barely have enough money left to get through the night until I leave for home tomorrow. You've got to pray for me tonight!"

My clothes were wet and sweat was running off my face. I was tired and weak physically. I tried to explain that, in this condition, I didn't have the faith to pray for her.

> *The truth of this woman's faith dawned on me. I said out loud, 'Thank God, You don't have to have perfect vessels to work Your miracles through.'*

Without turning my clothes loose, she cried, "I will not let you go until you pray for my healing!" I tried to pull loose, but her grip was tight.

Out of sheer exhaustion and frustration, I touched her forehead and cried, "Jesus, heal her."

To my utter surprise, she threw up her hands, weeping and rejoicing, praising God for His healing power going all through her. Without another word, she quickly walked away, leaving me astounded.

Back in my room, as I started to lie down, the still small voice said inside me, *"I healed her all right, but you won't get any credit for it."*

As I lay there reliving the scene, the truth of this woman's faith dawned on me. I said out loud, "Lord, I'll never fully understand Your ways. And thank God, You don't have to have perfect vessels to work Your miracles through."

As I pondered this more, I smiled to myself and said, "Why am I surprised? She was just *cashing in her receipt with God.*"

She had planted a big seed to get there, to hear the Word of God preached, to watch others getting healed, and to see that faith works in different ways. She knew that in her desperation, her faith (in spite of my lack of it at the moment) could be released, and what she had

> **When it looks like it's all over for any one of us, through our Seed-Faith, everything is possible.**

seeded for could be cashed in by the "bank of heaven" that was full of God's healing power.

Many times since, the Lord has brought this experience to my mind. I continue to marvel that when it looks like it's all over for any one of us, through our Seed-Faith, everything is possible.

I'm still seeing it happen all the time. I reached my 88th birthday on January 24, 2006, and I'm more excited than ever about my walk with Jesus and my Seed-Faith living. I just must remember to keep expecting the Lord of the harvest to multiply my seed sown, and to keep reminding everyone else to *expect a new miracle every day*.

I'll never forget the healing crusade in Miami, Florida. **There, a new phrase was revealed to me...and to the world.**

What I actually did in this situation was about to affect my life and ministry, and brought with it a further revelation of cashing in another receipt with God. There just may be something very personal and special in it for you.

IMPORTANT POINTS TO REMEMBER

1. This woman taught me the terrific power of determining to "cash in" one's receipt.

—What can stop us if we are determined to stand on our faith…if we refuse to let man stand in our way?

2. I believe she really understood in her spirit that expecting and going all out to cash in her receipt overcame me becoming the big obstacle.

—It reminds us of Galatians 6:9, "You shall reap if you don't give up."

CHAPTER TEN

The Bottom Line: Switching Our Minds From Our Seeding to Our Receipting

I desire fruit that may abound to your account.
—Philippians 4:17 KJV

For years in my giving, I never thought that with every gift (1) I was sowing a seed of my faith, (2) God was overseeing an account with personal receipts I was to cash out in time of need, and (3) we must switch gears from looking back at our seed sown to looking forward to God's "due season" to cash in our receipts. In other words, to look from the Lord of the seed to the Lord of the harvest, which are two different acts of our faith.

Paul said to the Philippians that he desired this—as fruit being produced—to *abound* to their account. Paul was writing by God's inspiration, telling us about God and His ways, His operating principles. Paul uses the word "abound." In Luke 6:38, Jesus uses the words "running over," to describe what He wants to follow our giving. David, in Psalm 23:5 KJV, uses the phrase, *My cup runneth over.* That means full, then overflowing with a surplus.

You see, in the beginning, no matter how much I gave myself to God or how much I poured myself into my giving, I always came out with less, not more. For me and my little family, and those I ministered to, there was no abounding, no running over, no surplus—exactly opposite from God and His ways, His operating principles.

How often I felt I was reduced and nothing was going to change. Yet, I carried God's calling on my life. Eventually, I had to start believing the Scriptures I was preaching and teaching, or give it up. So I finally came to that crucial point.

I saw I had to change because (1) I couldn't give up my faith, (2) I had to carry out God's calling on my life or be in disobedience, (3) if I didn't learn to switch gears from sowing to receiving, I would remain lacking in my Christian walk and in every area of my life.

Look at Philippians 4:17 again. Paul uses the words *"fruit to your account,"* meaning receipts the Lord God of heaven and earth Himself adds to your personal account. He deposits everything you give—money, time,

> **Eventually, I had to start believing the Scriptures I was preaching and teaching, or give it up.**

talent, sacrifice, devotion, prayer, or as they say, the whole nine yards.

I shudder to think I didn't know this. I lived and worked in an atmosphere in which I believed myself, and not the unfailing Word of God.

I think back to my banker, Mr. Beale, talking to me about the receipt he wrote to the trucker who had changed the tire for him on that cold, dark night.

From that hour, the trucker knew at all times he had a $200 receipt in his wallet. He knew when the right kind of need came along, he could go into that bank and cash it. Out of his giving of that good deed came his receiving, and he cashed it in at the point of his need.

Recently, I was sharing the truth of giving and receiving (receipting), of sowing and reaping, with a long-time good friend of ours, Samantha Landy, a Christian author and speaker, and long-time Partner of my ministry. When it dawned in her spirit that with all her giving she had fruit abounding to her account—receipts with God Himself—tears

> *He deposits everything you give—money, time, talent, sacrifice, devotion, prayer...the whole nine yards.*

flowed from her eyes. She grabbed her handkerchief and said, "Oral, is this really true?"

I said, "Samantha, read out loud verse 17 from the passage in Philippians 4:15-19."

She did.

I said, "Read it again."

Which she did.

I said, "Now paraphrase it to yourself."

She said, "Based on my giving, I have an account in heaven...according to the measure of the riches of Jesus Himself."

After she said these words out loud, she said, "Oral, I haven't been this excited in a long time. Let me ask you another question: Does my receiving apply to all my *past* giving from which I never expected to cash in my receipts?"

"Why not?" I said.

"Yes, why not?" she exclaimed.

And right then, she and Evelyn and I had a great time of rejoicing. I asked her to read verse 18, which is Paul's personal testimony: *But I have all, and abound: I am full, having received of Epaphroditus the things which were sent from you, an odour of a sweet smell, a sacrifice acceptable, well-pleasing to God* (KJV).

"Now," I said, "notice Paul said of himself, '*having received.*'"

A member of the Philippian group named Epaphroditus had carried the financial gift on a long journey—all the way to where Paul was in Rome. There the gift changed everything for Paul, just as cashing in our receipts changes things for us today.

Paul didn't mind testifying that he had cashed in his receipt with God on that occasion. What if he hadn't switched gears from his *giving* to his *receiving?*

We learn that Paul was not intimidated when he was in desperate need (vv. 10-13), or when he was blessed in times of overflowing prosperity (v. 18). He was simply living the Seed-Faith life, as Jesus said: *Give, and it shall be given unto you; good measure, pressed down, and shaken together, and running over, shall men give into your bosom. For with the same measure that ye mete withal it shall be measured to you again* (Luke 6:38 KJV).

Through living the Seed-Faith life, Paul was learning "the art of contentment" in good times and bad. He said he had learned to be content if he was abounding or overflowing, and also to be content if he was abased or in need. He was content because in whatever situation he was in, *he had a knowing* in his spirit that God was in control as the *Source* of his total supply. His real secret was in recognizing who his Source was at all times, then focusing his main attention, not on his prospering or his needfulness, but directly on the One who was giving him receipts for the sowing of his seed.

Paul learned to seek God and to plant his seed in order to find the answers, and to receive from the Lord of the harvest. I've had to do the same thing, for I, too, like all other believers I know, have rises and falls, highs and lows in my supply of things I have need of. I've had to learn in both good and bad times, and ups and downs, to be content with God, my Source.

If Paul couldn't get out of prison, then he chose to change things while in jail. To me, this means that I must continue to sow *and* to receive, and to believe for my harvest to come in one form or another—and never blame God for the bad things. For John 10:10 says the thief—or the devil—comes to steal, kill, and destroy, but Jesus gives us abundant life. So that settles it. To me, God is always a good God.

> **Paul learned to seek God and to plant his seed in order to find the answers, and to receive from the Lord of the harvest.**

At the last of his life, Paul knew he would cash in his receipt. Paul teaches us this in this 4th chapter of Philippians. Look at verse 10 KJV: *But I rejoiced in the Lord greatly, that now **at the last** your care of me hath **flourished** again; wherein ye were also careful, but ye **lacked opportunity**.*

In other words, all along his partners cared for him and his ministry, but were hindered in sending the supply. And Paul carefully reminded them that he didn't hold this against them, but pointed out that he "rejoiced greatly that your care of me has flourished again."

And how many times as we worked diligently to build and do all God asked of this ministry and of ORU did I feel the pain when we were not flourishing? I would remind God over and over that in order to educate thousands of young people and do all the other things we were called to do for His glory, I had to have help. I knew I

> *Living the Seed-Faith life is like breathing—truly a lifestyle, and one of never giving up.*

was committed to obeying the Lord, and I was faithfully sowing my seed. Now it was up to Him to check my receipt and impress upon me when it was my time to cash it in according to His riches in glory by Christ Jesus. But truthfully, it hasn't always been easy, and I'm convinced it never will be any easier until we literally get our believing right and follow through; until living the Seed-Faith life is like breathing—truly a lifestyle, and one of never giving up.

As Paul encouraged those he was writing to, I want to stop and encourage you to carry in your heart Galatians 6:9 KJV: *And let us not be weary in well doing: for in due season we shall reap, if we faint not.* I believe it is one of the keys to truly living a blessed life, filled with the constant, continuous rhythm of sowing and reaping, seedtime and harvest, giving and receipting.

Testimony
by Jere Melilli, M.D.

One particular time during our semi-annual meetings, the ORU Board of Regents had been in session all morning. The meeting had ended, and the Regents were leaving the meeting to have lunch. It was at this time that President Oral Roberts singled me out and indicated that he wished to speak to me alone. He revealed that God had spoken to him about my giving pattern.

"Jere," Oral said, "God has shown me that you take great joy in giving, but that you have difficulty in receiving."

He was absolutely correct in his statement. Since I had begun to prosper as a physician, it had become my practice to pay all of my current bills and give the rest to various ministries. It was a pleasure to do this because I felt God was pleased with my sincerity and generosity. I had little or no resources or savings.

Learning to receive

President Roberts then continued, "God wants you to have a harvest and to prosper. You're giving away your 'seed corn.' As you receive your harvest, God wants *you* to have a share in that harvest. When you do, it will not only bring security and abundance to you and your family, but will also enable you to give even more to the kingdom of God. Learn to receive and be blessed according to God's Word. God wants to do this for you!"

This encounter made me realize that God indeed wanted me not only to plant my seed, but to participate in His harvest, and to be blessed abundantly with all blessings. This has enabled me to bless not only my own life and practice, but to bless others even more than before. And it's continued every day of my life.

IMPORTANT POINTS TO REMEMBER

1. Ask yourself, as I did, "Am I willing and ready to switch over in my mind to the reality that I can cash in my receipts with God?"

2. Think about Samantha's question, "Can I cash in old receipts, my collected receipts…that I gave to the Lord of the seed, and then turn my mind and attention to receiving from the Lord of the harvest?"

3. Consider studying Philippians 4:13-19 often, and when you do, allow the same Holy Spirit who inspired the apostle Paul to write it, to inspire you in your understanding God's harvest for your life.

CHAPTER ELEVEN

Avoiding False Expectations

Several years ago, the chief of staff of the City of Faith Medical Center, which we had built across from ORU, told me they had a serious problem with a patient who said she was pregnant.

"Our obstetricians have carefully examined her, and although she has symptoms that she is pregnant, we know from a medical standpoint her expectations are false. She's told us she will leave only if you come and pray with her, and tell her she has false expectations." What an unusual position to be put in the middle of!

"Look," I said, "I'm not a doctor."

"We know that, but she thinks because you built the City of Faith, you will know whether she's pregnant or not. She's been in her hospital room for seven days now and won't leave. Only you can help us deal with this."

> *As I went with the doctor into her room, I wasted no time in looking to God as the Source of all knowledge.*

Well, OK, I thought.

As I was driving over to see her, I prayed, "Lord, how will I know how to deal with this? I know very little about the medical side of this."

In my spirit I heard the Lord say, "She's not pregnant. She has let herself get deceived by false pretenses. You will know, too, when you pray for her, and she will see that when I called you to merge my healing streams of medicine and prayer, she can accept the doctors' diagnosis. I will guide you in this."

As I went with the doctor into her room, I wasted no time in laying my hands on her head and looking to God as the Source of all knowledge. Immediately I knew—not medically, but in my spirit—something was not real here. I felt a falseness, and I said to her in the name of Jesus, "My sister, our doctors have agreed after all their tests that you are not pregnant. I want you to get up out of this bed and go home. And I pray the Lord to bless you."

She looked at me and said, "Well, all right, I'll do it." And she did! Because her spirit now had a knowing of the truth.

My next step was to sit down with our doctors. "Tell me," I said, "what is a false pregnancy?"

Our chief obstetrician said, "The medical term for false pregnancy is pseudocyesis, or phantom pregnancy. This woman had all the symptoms of pregnancy except for the presence and products of conception. This condition is marked by abdominal swelling and other symptoms of pregnancy. It is psychosomatic in origin and exhibits changes in the hormonal balance of pregnancy."

I said, "Doctor, in other words, no seed has been implanted in her womb?"

"That's right," he replied.

I said, "Are you saying that medically, the desire

for a child can actually grow so intense that it can give false expectations?"

He said, "I'm afraid so. We in the field of healing through medicine see this from time to time. We find it extremely difficult after full diagnosis to convince the person that, while we understand, she must face up to this illusion. In this case, this very nice woman wouldn't believe us, and because she believed in your prayers, she had to have a word from the Lord through you."

Believe me, I learned something most important that day about the *negative* side of expecting a harvest: That is, unless the seed of faith is actually sown, it is false, and can even become extreme defeatism in one's personal life.

Over the years, I've thought about the seed more and more. According to God, there is no substitute for seed and the actual sowing of it. *Everything comes from a seed* that has been planted, either of this earth or in the spiritual realm.

I saw John 3:16 KJV in a totally new light: *For God so loved the world, that he gave his only begotten Son, that whosoever believeth in him should not perish, but have everlasting life.*

I had preached on John 3:16 many times, marveling at God's love for the whole world in every generation. But I had missed what made up the giving of His Son Jesus on the Cross. I had read in the Bible that Jesus was

> *According to God, there is no substitute for seed and the actual sowing of it. Everything comes from a seed that has been planted.*

referred to as God's seed, and God was sowing that seed into the earth to get back the human race that He had lost after creating them.

In the very beginning, the sin of Adam and Eve, our forefathers, allowed satan to deceive them and cause rebellion against the Creator. God had said to the devil:

> *Because thou hast done this, thou art cursed above all cattle, and above every beast of the field; upon thy belly shalt thou go, and dust shalt thou eat all the days of thy life: and I will put enmity between thee and the woman, and between thy seed and her seed; it shall bruise thy head, and thou shalt bruise his heel* (Genesis 3:14-15 KJV).

The "seed of the woman" referred to the Messiah—Jesus—whom God would send to redeem man from his sin. Then God said, "As long as the earth remains, there shall be seedtime and harvest." (Genesis 8:22). Again He said the Messiah would be "the seed of David" (Romans 1:3; 2 Timothy 2:8). Peter called Jesus "the incorruptible seed" (1 Peter 1:23), the seed to be planted by God on the Cross to show us the way to "believe on Him and not perish" (John 3:16).

The revelation of Jesus being **the Seed of God the Father** gradually came to me in a simple way that I could understand. It was like I was hearing God say,

> *I am a seed of the Lord. And I can choose to sow my every act of giving as a seed of my faith.*

"I am lonely. I miss My family," and Jesus saying, "Father, You have made Me the Seed of redemption for Your lost family. I know the price I will have to pay on the Cross to restore Your family to You, but send Me, sow Me out of Your love and faith and hope. And as You do, You can expect to receive back Your family as Your harvest."

It was at that point that I began to understand

about the power of God's love, His faith, and His hope, the three things the apostle Paul declares are the greatest of all, according to 1 Corinthians 13:13.

For God so loved that He *gave* first. He believed in me first. He had hope for me first. He included loving the whole world first.

It broke me up.

He so loved…

That He gave…

His best seed…His only begotten Son…

Raising Jesus from the dead in the resurrection.

Then He expected the miracle harvest of the salvation of each of us in return. That is His faith. And then making His faith a seed—and certainly His best seed—that I, or anyone who would believe, would not perish, but would forever be a part of the family He loved. If I believed, I would not perish, but I would have eternal life!

And God is still receiving His harvest in every soul saved.

The flood of joy that flowed over me is still inside me, reminding me that I am part of God's seed He sowed for my salvation, and propelling me with the Gospel to this day.

I now know I am a seed of the Lord. And I can choose to sow my every act of giving as a seed of my faith, just as God did.

I can choose to plant my seed with sure expectations, not false ones like the woman believing to bear a child when she had no seed in her. It's simple—no seed, no harvest. No receipt…no cashing it in with God.

How many times before I got into Seed-Faith had I expected God to intervene miraculously in my life—but because of no seed sown, I was left disappointed. Now, because of my obedience to seed sowing and receipting, I can partake of His promise to "supply all my needs according to His riches in glory by Christ Jesus" (Philippians 4:19).

IMPORTANT POINTS TO REMEMBER

1. Remember, we cannot rely on illusion in expecting a harvest from our seed.

—Seed not planted cannot reproduce.

—Giving nothing—even if God multiplies it—is still nothing, just more of it.

2. When my need is greatest, I start questioning myself, "When did I sow my last seed? Have I actually been sowing my seed?"

—Sowing your seed is the only way to order your harvest in advance.

—You must switch gears and go from dwelling on your seed sown over to looking to God your Source, the Lord of the harvest, to bring you your harvest.

3. The woman had false expectations for a baby—no seed had been sown. But with seed sown, we can live in both seeding and harvesting…we can live in God's reward system (Philippians 4:17, Hebrews 11:6).

CHAPTER TWELVE

Please Meet My Friend Louie

A s I was finishing writing this little book, a golfing friend came to my door and asked for a few minutes with me. He had had a lot of fun telling the others in our golfing foursome what he called "Oral Roberts stories." He knew all the latest ones, and I had enjoyed them.

But when he stopped by, he wasn't telling any funny stories. He was deadly serious.

"Oral," he said, "I'm in trouble. I'm empty. And

the older I get, it's getting worse." The strain on his face was excruciating to see.

I knew him to have been highly successful in building a great pizza company, and a few years ago, he had sold it for millions of dollars, "to live a little," as he referred to it.

On the golf course, everything looked great. He was the life of our group.

> *The God I serve is a good God. He's for us and has something good for us to fill that empty heart and to turn the light of life— real life—back on.*

As usual, on the golf course I don't preach my religion. I play to relax, for recreation, for my health, so that I can do my work better later. So I was surprised he was telling me all this.

"Louie," I said, "how can I help you?"

"My wife's divorced me. I gave her half the money and our home. And of course, I still have plenty left. My children are married, with families, and doing all right. I've had lots of friendships, but," he pointed to his heart, "right here, Preacher, the light has gone out."

Putting his head down, he sighed and said, "God, I'm so empty."

What was coming up in my spirit was no long sermon and no spirit of condemnation. The God I serve is a good God. He's for us and has something good for us to fill that empty heart and to turn the light of life—real life—back on. I was thinking of the seed, the miracle of Seed-Faith.

"Louie, my friend, I imagine you have sown a lot of good seed," I said, but before I could finish, he interrupted me and said, "That's my problem—I don't have any good seed planted." His eyes teared, and I've seldom seen such a lost look on a person's face.

"But you know something about the Lord or you wouldn't have told me this. Isn't that right?" I asked.

He looked straight into my eyes. "Yes, I do. But I'm a lapsed Christian. Now I know I must give up my false expectations. I've got to come to the Man Himself. I'm 67 years old, and I've got to do it *now*."

We joined hands and prayed. I gave him two little books, *The Prayer of Jabez,* by Bruce Wilkinson, and one of mine, *The Miracle of Seed-Faith*, the first of the Seed-Faith books that I wrote years ago. And I left it at that, just trusting that God would come alive in his heart.

Recently I saw Louie again, and I asked, "How are you now?"

He told me, "I've got those two little books on my bed table. I've got both almost read."

The look I had seen on his face the last time wasn't there as much, I noticed. I looked into his eyes and smiled, and a smile started on his face.

"I've got some new seed in now," he told me. "I'm not so empty anymore."

"Well," I said, "I'm just sending my final book to the printer, *Cashing In Your Receipt With God.*"

"Yeah," he replied. "When I was with you, you told me about one of the chapters where you cashed in one of your receipts and got healed of appendicitis. I've told some friends about that. Some laughed, but others believed it. I believed it so much I'd like to read the whole book. I'd like to cash in some receipts myself."

And at the end of the conversation, I realized that the feeling I had in my heart for Louie is no longer for a man who has no seed in and no receipts with the Lord of the harvest. But it is now for one who finally found how he could get on God's reward system of seedtime and harvest, sowing and reaping, giving and receipting.

My Prayer for You

Dear Reader,
The Lord bless you,
May you hearken to His voice,
And walk His path.
He will surely walk it with you.

Your friend,
Oral Roberts

THE GREATEST MIRACLE OF ALL

The greatest miracle of all is the miracle of being born again. That miracle is available to each one of us when we sincerely repent of our sins, ask God's forgiveness, and receive His Son, Jesus, as our personal Lord and Savior. If you've never surrendered your life to God, or if you've turned away from God and you want to return to Him, now is the time…God is waiting for you. His arms are open wide to receive you. Just pray this simple prayer right now:

O Lord, be merciful to me, a sinner. I realize that I've been wrong, and I'm sorry. I repent of every sin, every wrongdoing, and I ask Your forgiveness. I receive Jesus Christ, Your only begotten Son, as my Lord and my Savior. I believe that Jesus went to the Cross for me and paid the price for my salvation, and now I take Him into my heart. I return to my heavenly Father. I declare that I am born again. I am a child of God. Old sins are gone, and I have a brand-new life in Christ.

In Jesus' name. Amen.

If you confess with your mouth Jesus as Lord, and believe in your heart that God raised Him from the dead, you will be saved; for with the heart a person believes, resulting in righteousness, and with the mouth he confesses, resulting in salvation.

—Romans 10:9-10 NASB

When you need prayer
anytime day or night,
we're here for you!

The Abundant Life
Prayer Group

918.495.7777

I would love to hear from you...

I would love to hear from you, but even more than that, I would love to pray for you and write you back. I hope you'll let me know what you're believing for so we can join together in agreement and turn our faith loose for miracles!

–Richard Roberts

Send your prayer requests to me by:

- **writing: Richard Roberts, Tulsa, OK 74171,**
- **e-mailing: prayer@orm.cc,**
- **logging on to: www.orm.cc, or**
- **calling the Abundant Life Prayer Group at 918-495-7777.**

IT'S ABOUT YOU @ **ORU**

FACE THE FACTS

Which facts? How about more than 280 professors, most with doctorates? Or classroom ratios of 16 students to every instructor? At ORU you'll work 1:1 with dedicated faculty who are at the top of their fields—Christian mentors who listen, guide your thinking and challenge you to break new intellectual ground. You'll love it. That's a fact.

- 61 undergraduate majors
- 14 master's programs
- 2 doctoral programs
- Small classes
- Students from over 60 countries
- Financial aid available to most students

Come visit us for our next College Weekend

It's all about you.
Find out why.
www.oru.edu or 800-678-8876